Earthwatch

Today's World in Space

Earthwatch

By David Baker

Rourke Enterprises, Inc.
Vero Beach, FL 32964

Library of Congress Cataloging-in-Publication Data
Baker, David , 1944-
   Earthwatch/by David Baker.
   p. cm. — (Today's world in space)
   Includes index.
   Summary: Explores the development and applications of military and civilian satellites designed to observe the earth and send back information about land and inland water areas, vegetation and crops, violent storms and dangerous weather, and nuclear activities.
   ISBN 0-86592-372-8
   1. Remote sensing — Juvenile literature. [1. Artificial satellites.]
I. Title. II. Series: Baker, David, 1944- Today's world in space.
G70.4.B35   1989   88-33691
621.36'78 · dc19   CIP
                                                       AC

CONTENTS

Eyes in the Sky

People have been watching things on the ground from a great height for more than a hundred years. Union balloon aviators in the Civil War (1861-65) spied on Confederate troops to learn about their maneuvers prior to battle. In World War One (1914-18), planes were used for reconnaissance and spotting for the guns. With the aid of a simple radio telephone, observers would peer over the side of the plane and report to the gun batteries on the accuracy of their artillery fire. It was a dangerous practice from low altitude, since the shell sometimes went higher than the planes could fly.

Before World War Two began in 1939, the United States operated several aircraft carriers in the Pacific Ocean. The U.S. Navy wanted to know if any potential enemy ships were nearby, but they had difficulty with spotting them in the vast ocean. There was no way of seeing the entire Pacific, and aircraft were the only real means of spotting enemy ships. Information gathered by pilots was sent to Washington, D.C., for analysis. Nevertheless, when the Japanese attacked Pearl Harbor without warning on Sunday, December 7, 1941, it was a total surprise.

During World War Two, the United States

In the early part of this century, German engineers built giant airships to observe the ground from high altitude and gain information about potential enemy activity.

6

Planes like this developed quickly during World War One for spying and gathering information about troop movements.

developed airborne reconnaissance to aid the army and the navy and to support bombing and airborne attack missions. The value of photo-reconnaissance, using cameras to take pictures of activity on the ground, was immense. Good intelligence information helped battle commanders plan their action, and it helped politicians understand the state of the enemy's forces and their ability to continue fighting.

After the war ended in 1945, the United States developed several aircraft that could be used to maintain watch on countries potentially hostile to America and its allies. Almost every part of the globe was being mapped by long-range reconnaissance planes, just in case U.S. forces had to go to the aid of a small country and fight on foreign soil. At the end of the war, maps were not particularly accurate, and the use of long-range bombers converted into mapping planes was a great advantage.

The most spectacular reconnaissance plane was the Convair RB-36. It had six enormous propeller engines and four jet engines. The jet engines were used to take off and gain height, and the propeller engines were used for most of the long-distance flying. Developments in

aviation had made possible around-the-world flights on an almost routine basis.

When Pearl Harbor was attacked in 1941, the best bomber in service had a range of just over 2,000 miles. Ten years later, the RB-36 could stay in the air for more than two days and fly more than 13,000 miles non-stop. It carried up to 28 crew members who would take shifts manning the fourteen cameras, sleeping in their off-duty hours in special bunks at the the back of the plane.

Developed in the 1950s as the U-2 spy plane, the Lockheed TR-1 is today a tactical reconnaissance aircraft, carrying a wide range of cameras and other electronic sensors.

The RB-36 could get up to a height of about 45,000 feet. Some made it well above 50,000 feet on reconnaissance missions for the U.S. Air Force. The plane was expensive to operate, however, and it was withdrawn from service in 1959. It was outdated, and its replacement was

After World War Two, the United States developed this super reconnaissance bomber, the RB-36.

Packed with many different types of reconnaissance cameras, the RB-36 was able to gather vast quantities of data about all regions of the Earth.

9

The TR-1 is not armed, and exists purely to look down at the Earth and gather information.

considerably better. The RB-36 was followed by two very different airplanes that carried out distinctly separate duties.

One, called the U-2, performed a general reconnaissance duty, routinely observing potentially interesting activity in foreign countries. The other, called the SR-71, made specific reconnaissance flights to investigate sudden and potentially hostile activity. The U-2 appeared in 1955 and was operated by the *Central Intelligence Agency (CIA)* on missions that included spy flights high over the Soviet Union. It was slow but could reach altitudes of more than 70,000 feet. This was far higher than most ground-to-air missiles could reach in those days.

Another type of Earth observation plane is the Lockheed SR-71 Blackbird reconnaissance jet, which is capable of flying at around 2,300 MPH.

The other plane, the much more revolutionary SR-71, was capable of speeds greater than 2,000 MPH for long distances. It could outrun any combat plane in the world, and still can. The SR-71 came into service with the U.S. Air Force during 1966 and has proved a valuable reconnaissance plane for more than 20 years. Like the U-2 and the RB-36 before it, the SR-71 is not armed and relies on sheer speed to escape interception.

In the 1950s, the cameras and the technology provided clear, high-resolution pictures of targets on the ground from as far as fourteen miles up. *Resolution* is a term photographers use to describe the amount of

The Lockheed SR-71 has broken many speed records, and although it was designed more than 25 years ago it is still the world's fastest plane.

detail visible in a photograph. It refers to the minimum distance between two points of light that can be seen as separate spots without merging together as one. Camera systems used in the RB-36 could "resolve" objects only a few feet in size.

The High Ground

Generals have always wanted to fight wars from "the high ground." This was usually the highest hilltop around that gave the best view of the enemy and the place the battle was to be fought. In peace time, too, it helps to have the high ground. From a tall hill you can watch the activities of your potential enemy and see what defenses he is building, what preparations he is making for war, and how he is moving his troops around.

In the 1950s, the U.S. Air Force began a secret program to use the highest ground of all — space. The air force's success with airborne camera planes and missions that carried the giant RB-36 all over the world led to a new mission — getting outside the atmosphere and taking a global look. This reconnaissance mission would not be challenged by potential adversaries, and cameras would be safe from attack. It was to be achieved with satellites.

Plans were made to put a camera in a special rocket stage being developed in the early 1950s. Built by Lockheed and called Agena, this rocket would not launch itself into *orbit*. That job would be done by a big missile, Thor, being designed

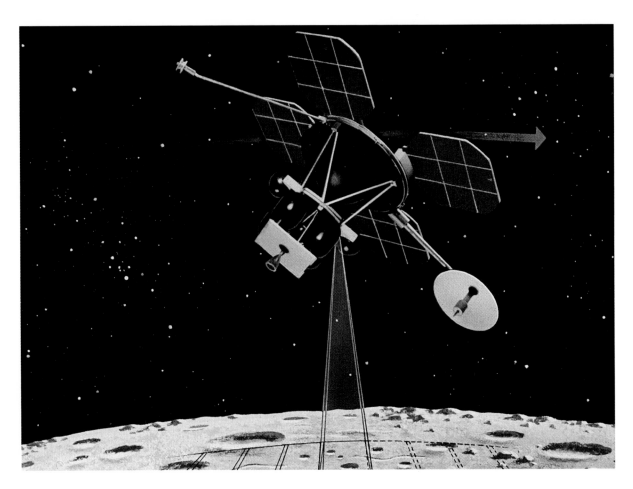

Early camera systems sent into space on Earth-orbiting satellites were able to process film on board, as was the NASA lunar orbiter, sent to map the moon in the mid-1960s.

12

An early Earth observation satellite, *Samos 2* is prepared for launch at Vandenberg
Air Force Base in January 1961.

by Douglas (now McDonnell Douglas). Thor was big and powerful by the standards of the 1950s and still remains a workhorse for the American space program. It was to put in space a camera system attached to the Agena rocket stage, and this camera would routinely watch the surface as the Earth slowly revolved.

The satellite was to be put into *polar orbit* where the path of the satellite goes over the north pole and the south pole at right-angles to the equator. Since the Earth revolves in a counter-clockwise direction when viewed from the north pole, the path of the satellite would remain more or less fixed. The Earth would slowly spin underneath the satellite so that every day the cameras on the satellite would view approximately the same strip of land below.

Each orbit would last about 90 minutes. This is the time it takes the satellite to circle around the Earth at orbital speed for a low orbit. The satellite had to be high enough to orbit the Earth in a near vacuum; otherwise, the atmosphere would slow it down. The minimum height is about 100 miles, although it is possible for a satellite to dip down as low as 50 miles for a couple of orbits without being slowed sufficiently to fall back to Earth. At 100 miles high with an orbital speed of 17,500 MPH, the satellite takes 90 minutes to go once around the planet.

Clearly, the air force wanted the satellite to orbit as slowly as possible to give the cameras the best resolution. The closer to the ground, the better the picture. At a height of 100 miles, the cameras would get good views and the satellite would not be unduly affected by the traces of atmosphere that exist at that height. Nevertheless, an orbit of 100 miles was about 10 times farther away from Earth than the operating height of the RB-36 and other camera-carrying planes, and it was seven times the picture-taking altitude of the U-2 when it appeared.

The *Discoverer* space capsule returns to Earth carrying valuable film shot from space.

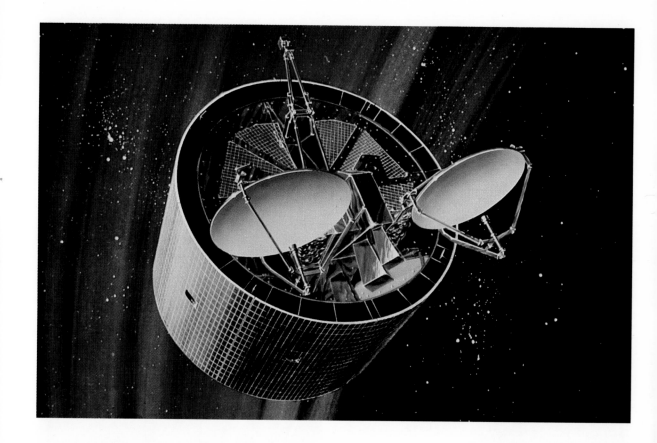

Today, satellite pictures and information about the Earth are relayed back to the United States via communications satellites in space.

The advantages, however, were enormous. Nations could not protest about camera-carrying machines flying over their territory. National jurisdiction ended at the edge of the atmosphere. For the cost of one launch, a satellite could be made to operate for several months, and perhaps years. It would take pictures anytime it was told to over any location on Earth. Moreover, it would return regularly to cover the same areas on Earth, providing a continuous watch on new buildings going up, military base construction, and the number and type of ships moving in or out of ports and harbors.

The air force had to decide what type of camera to use in the satellite. In previous surveillance work, the cameras, the film, and the photographer returned to tell intelligence people about the area of interest and to comment on things the cameras failed to find. The photographer's eyes sometimes glimpsed things that were gone before the camera could take pictures. With a satellite there would be no way to tinker with the camera, point it at things that suddenly looked interesting, or return the film to Earth easily.

The air force finally settled on two different kinds of cameras. One could take film and return it to Earth for processing and analysis, and the other worked like a TV camera, sending images down on a radio signal. The film system would yield pictures with clear and precise detail, but the size of the roll of film was limited and only a certain number of pictures could be taken by each satellite. Pictures from the TV system would not be as clear, but the camera would, in theory, continue to operate simply and cheaply from space.

15

satellite in space. Other people in the United States had been working on launching a satellite for the scientific study of space, but the Soviets beat everyone, launching their satellite in October 1957.

Discoverer consisted of a rocket stage, a camera-carrying module, and a capsule that would return to Earth with the film. As the capsule fell back, it would be tracked by radar, and planes from Hawaii would fly out to meet it. The plan was that the plane would snatch the capsule as it fell through the air by using a large wire held out in front. The wire would snag the capsule, and it would be wound in by an operator on the plane.

Giant launch vehicles like this Titan routinely place complex and weighty spy satellites into orbit.

Military satellites are vulnerable to attack because they are delicate structures that use sensitive solar cells to convert sunlight into electrical power.

The air force developed the two systems side by side, although work on the film camera progressed more quickly because it was a more familiar technology. The first camera-carrying satellite was called *Discoverer*. It was not the first

16

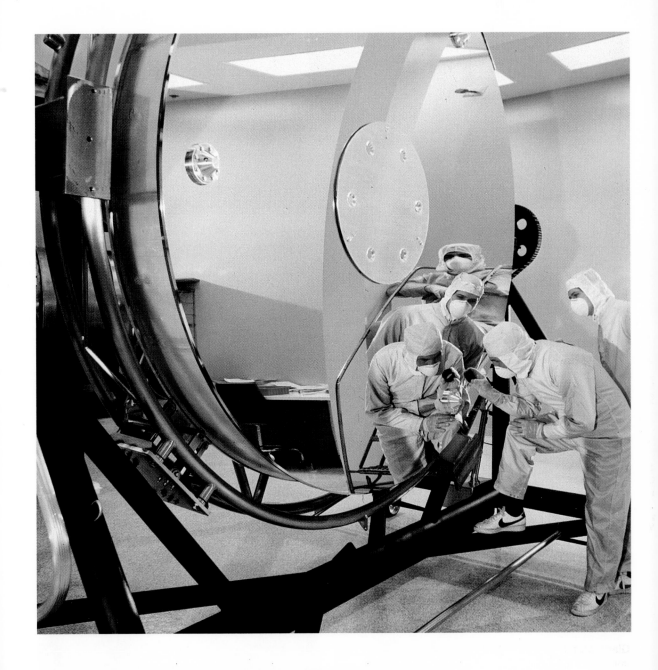

Mirrors like this one, being built for NASA's Hubble Space Telescope, are carried by spy satellites to enlarge the image of objects on the ground.

The Discoverer series was not all that successful, but it led the way to bigger and better spy satellites. Soon, great improvements had been made in the technology, and TV cameras were used to get pictures on what intelligence experts call a "real-time" basis. This means that they receive the picture almost at the same instant it is taken, which cuts down delay and the risk that something will go wrong with the recovery process.

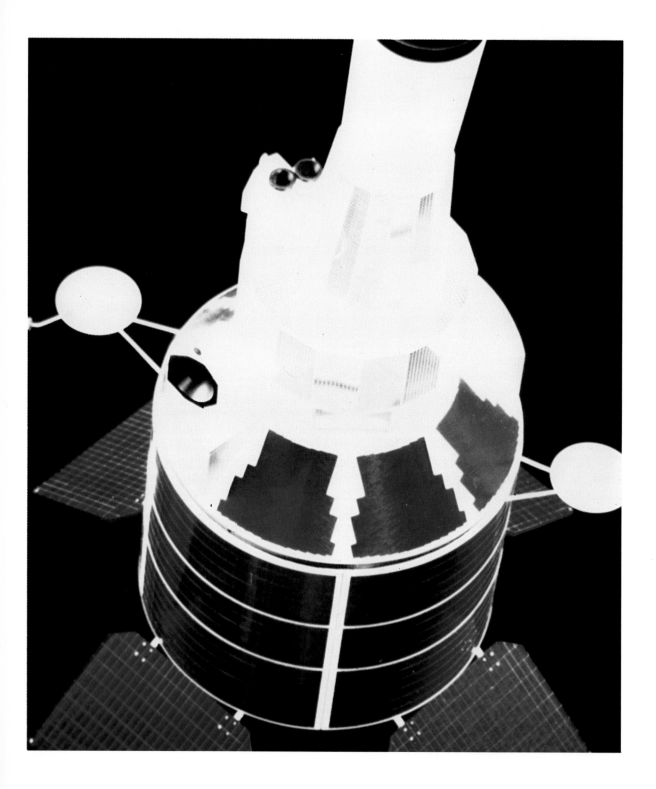

Satellites like the one shown here are put into space to observe activity on the Earth and to watch for signs of a surprise nuclear attack.

The Hubble Space Telescope, developed for astronomers to observe the universe, is very similar to the more powerful reconnaissance satellites used by the United States to observe military activity in foreign countries.

This specially developed mirror design from the spy satellite program is being developed for use as a possible reflector for laser beams on anti-missile spacecraft.

By the end of the 1960s, both the U.S. and the Soviet Union had made great strides in developing a complete range of camera-carrying satellites. The Soviets used their Vostok capsule, which had been designed to carry cosmonauts into space, as an unmanned camera-carrying spacecraft. With this they could use huge cameras and lots of film. Generally, the U.S. went for special satellites with long operating periods in orbit. The Soviets were not as quick to perfect the picture recovery technique and had to bring the entire spacecraft back before they could get at the film.

Spy satellites began to play a vital role in defense and politics. With uncertain information from the occasional airplane flight over Soviet territory, political leaders in Washington over-estimated the Soviet build-up of missiles and rockets. When satellites began to return more detailed and consistent pictures, the United States realized that they had a distinct advantage in nuclear weapons and long-range rockets. This was the first recognition that spy satellites were productive and that they could provide information that might stop excess expenditure on unnecessary arms.

Orbital Eyes

Two major boosts to space reconnaissance occurred in the 1960s. The first manned spacecraft was launched, enabling humans to look at targets on Earth for the first time. In addition, a broad range of other military "eyes" were put into space. The human eyeball is a wondrous thing, and connected to a human brain it is unique. No machine can perform as well as a human can. During the first several years of space reconnaissance, the absence of human eyes from space led several people to believe that cameras and instruments could do a better job. After all, the human eye does not have a telephoto lens, and the satellite camera does.

When the first astronauts went into orbit, they were confined to small capsules with little opportunity to look around. They certainly couldn't get a good, long look at the Earth below. The Mercury capsule that carried the first four American astronauts into space between 1962 and 1963 had one small window directly in front, but it was not adequate for Earth observation. When the two-man Gemini came along in 1965, it provided the first real chance to look at the planet below.

This Skylab view of south-east Louisiana was taken using a special infra-red camera. It shows the Mississippi river flowing south through the picture from Baton Rouge at the top to the western suburbs of New Orleans.

Shot by astronauts during 1975, this picture of the eastern Mediterranean area shows all of Lebanon and portions of Israel, Egypt, Syria, and Jordan.

What the astronauts reported greatly surprised everyone. Some astronauts could see locomotives on rail tracks. Others could pick up the trail of pleasure boats in the Gulf of Mexico. A few even saw passenger planes flying around in the atmosphere one hundred miles below. A number of astronauts were reluctant to tell about the things they could see for fear the doctors would think they were *hallucinating* and take them off flight duty!

The astronauts' story could not be kept secret for long. Much was visible from space, and one could use an ordinary hand-held camera to take stunning pictures of great value to many people.

Military officials and civilian scientists all over the world clamored to get the pictures from Gemini. Flights up to two weeks in duration gave astronauts ample time to get large numbers of amazing shots, and geologists found fascinating and important features on the planet they did not know existed before the manned missions.

This breath-taking view of parts of Peru and Bolivia in South America clearly shows a part of the Andes mountain range through the unpolluted atmosphere of this remote region.

NASA began a study of what manned spacecraft could do from orbit, and scientific study of the planet through photographs was high on the list. For much of the 1960s, the manned space program was preoccupied with Project Apollo. Set up by President Kennedy to put astronauts on the moon by the end of the decade, Apollo provided the big rockets and the large spacecraft to build a big manned space station in orbit. Skylab, launched in 1973, was the first and last time Apollo equipment was used for this purpose, but it proved the importance of humans in space using powerful cameras with high-quality film.

In one example, the astronauts in space were asked to point the camera at Mali in central Africa to search for places where the local tribes

Showing up as a thin white line from top-right to middle-left on this picture of central Africa, an abandoned canal built to bring water to starving tribes is seen in this shuttle picture.

could find water. Mali was hit by a sudden drought, and the nomads were dying of thirst and lack of food. The Skylab pictures were returned to Earth and quickly processed, giving officials precise information so they could show the nomads where to find water. The astronauts found areas that looked promising and the cameras could detect folds in the land that were guaranteed to contain water just below the surface.

Many different applications arose from the space pictures. Geologists used them to look for new fuel and mineral resources. The view from space took in wide areas, and features that could not be seen from the low-flying altitude of a light plane stood out clearly from space. Mapping became a simple and cost-effective exercise with pictures from space. Egypt was one of the first to use space pictures to help update the scientific study of water resources and geologic features.

While the awareness of what space photographs could be used for widened, the military spy satellites had contributed a few new ideas themselves. Programmed to take pictures on a regular basis, spy satellites were just as likely to take pictures over cloud-filled skies as across wide expanses of cloudless territory. Military weather satellites that were launched in the 1960s provided information about weather conditions around the world. The military began

The snow-covered north-west corner of Wyoming seen from Skylab, with Yellowstone Lake just left of center, Yellowstone National Park to the south-west, the extended range of the Big Horn Mountains due east, and the Wind River Range at bottom center.

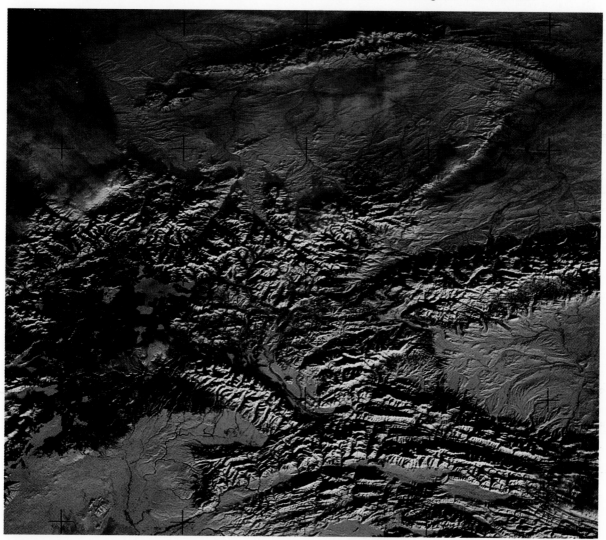

25

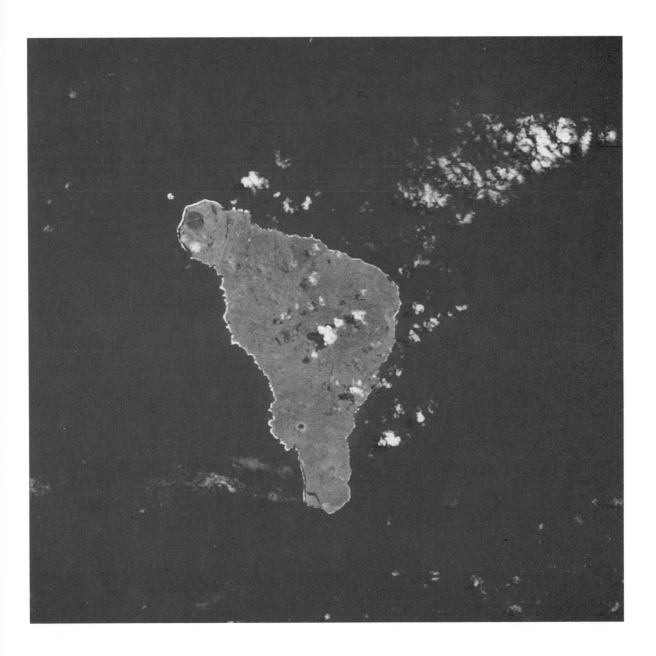

Seen here during a shuttle mission in 1985, and best known for its huge heads carved by natives and directed to stare out to sea, Easter Island is located over 2,000 miles from the Pacific coast of Chile in South America.

to use information from these satellites to predict the best areas to photograph free of cloud or bad weather. This saved film and improved the efficiency of the satellites in space.

Other satellites were eventually brought into use for navigation and military communications. Rather than observing the Earth, these satellites remained in space as beacons through which users could improve existing activities. Navigation with satellites was better than alternative methods and gave improved accuracy. Communication via satellite provided a worldwide service for the first time. Developments in these fields would also be used for civilian purposes.

Another form of observation arose from the need to watch for signs of surprise attack. With Pearl Harbor in mind, the military found great security in the ability to watch constantly for the unexpected launch of long-range nuclear missiles. These *early-warning satellites* were placed in space to watch large areas of the Earth where missiles might be launched from. They watched the vast interior of the Soviet Union and areas of the ocean where Soviet missile-launching submarines hid.

Photographs from space can help geologists detect features impossible to see from the ground; here, ancient and previously unknown volcanoes have been discovered in South America.

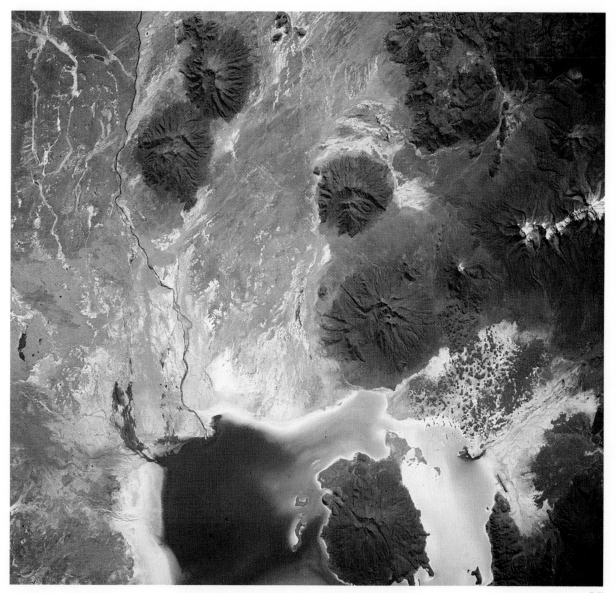

Space pictures are being used to help scientists understand how rock formations have changed over millions of years; this picture shows the Mountains of Tibet, the most remote region in the world, where no point in the picture is less than 14,000 feet above sea level.

Spy and weather satellites are in relatively low orbits, but the need to watch certain areas of the Earth continuously required a satellite to remain fixed over one spot. There is only one way that can happen from space. By placing a satellite 22,300 miles out above the equator, the time it takes the satellite to go once around the Earth is exactly the time it takes the Earth to spin once on its axis. Because the satellite and the Earth are both moving at the same pace, the satellite can stare down at one location all the time.

Early-warning satellites carry special sensors to watch for the hot rocket exhaust of a *ballistic missile* being launched. In this way, the satellite can give warning of attack even as the missile is climbing into the sky from its launch pad. Other satellites similar to early-warning satellites have been developed and launched to watch for signs of nuclear explosions on the surface of the Earth. The satellites monitor an international agreement to ban all nuclear tests in the atmosphere.

Nobody expects the Americans or the Soviets to break that agreement, but other smaller countries might. Not everyone has signed such an agreement. Because nuclear weapons have such devastating power, it is important to know who has nuclear weapons and who does not. The monitoring satellites help police the planet and warn of new developments. In this positive way, satellites can help maintain international agreements and improve the relationships between nations. Like the police officer on the street, the presence of the satellite alone could deter a country from testing its nuclear weapon in the atmosphere.

People who want to understand how the sea affects coastlines use pictures like this of sand dunes along the Namib Desert shoreline, a coastal region of south-west Africa, where many ships were lost.

Landsat

By the end of the 1960s, the use of space for observing the Earth had taken on new importance, While the military continued to improve the quality of spy cameras and the satellites that carried them, other people wanted to open up space photography for wide public use. The advantages were simply too great to restrict to a few. The military satellites were a top secret program. No one, not even the President, admitted they actually existed. They were referred to as "national technical means," but everybody knew what that meant.

The first observation satellite for public use was developed by NASA, the National Aeronautics and Space Administration, during the late 1960s. NASA had been formed in 1958 to look after the nation's non-military space projects and wanted to exploit the new opportunitities. There was much that could be seen from space that would help farmers, tree growers, town planners, fishermen, and a host of other people doing ordinary jobs.

Using space to observe the Earth with advanced camera systems is called *remote sensing*. It covers the observation of the planet and its resources and aims to provide information that no other system could provide.

This view of the Andes mountains separating Chile and Argentina helps geologists understand the difference between surface features formed by volcanoes and those formed in other ways.

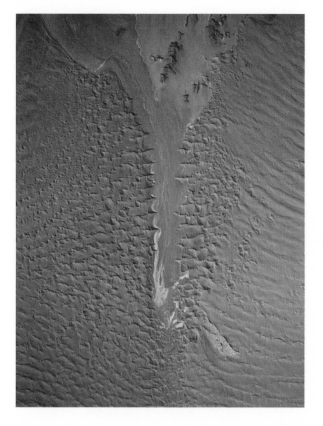

different types of vegetation and the areas where some patches were diseased or dying. It displays a contrast between natural surfaces, such as soil and living things, and artificial structures, such as houses and buildings. This helps town planners see the extent of their building work and clearly shows areas of natural beauty threatened by over-planning.

The infra-red pictures show clearly the distinction between land and water. Water and moist areas on land show up as dark patches. Dry land areas are very bright, looking like snow does to the naked eye. These pictures help scientists understand the balance between wet and dry areas. Wetlands are important for natural life and help keep vegetation strong and fertile. Such mapping of wet and dry areas can warn scientists of dry periods and impending droughts.

Sand dunes from space; flash floods can cut through the beautifully formed structures.

NASA scientists developed a camera that was actually three cameras strapped together taking pictures at exactly the same time. Each of the three cameras had a special lens that was sensitive to a particular color. One camera took pictures in red, one in blue-green, and a third in *infra-red*.

The infra-red color, while not visible to the human eye, is very important for getting information about the health of crops on the ground. This three-color camera system was to be carried into space on a Landsat satellite, which was also equipped with a second instrument. This was called the *multi-spectral scanner*, or *MSS*. It, too, had several lenses that would take pictures simultaneously. Two lenses shot pictures in visible light, and two shot pictures in infra-red.

The blue-green light picture penetrates shallow water. It would, for instance, show detail on the sea floor in areas like the Bahamas. The red light lens would distinguish between

The brightness of vegetation changes according to the type of vegetation being observed. For instance, big leaves appear brighter than small leaves. Such information helps identify the kind of tree or bush being seen from space. The cameras would be unable to pick out the size of the leaf from an ordinary picture, but the level of brightness in the scanner will provide that information. Hardwood trees show up brighter than pine trees, and tobacco leaves are brighter than wheat.

By using different lens systems and cameras, it becomes possible to get information about the surface of the Earth impossible to obtain by other means. If people were employed to cover the ground and get the same information, it would take thousands of people several years to achieve the results available from one Landsat picture. No wonder people everywhere were eagerly awaiting the results from Landsat when it was launched in July 1972.

The Landsat results were everything that had

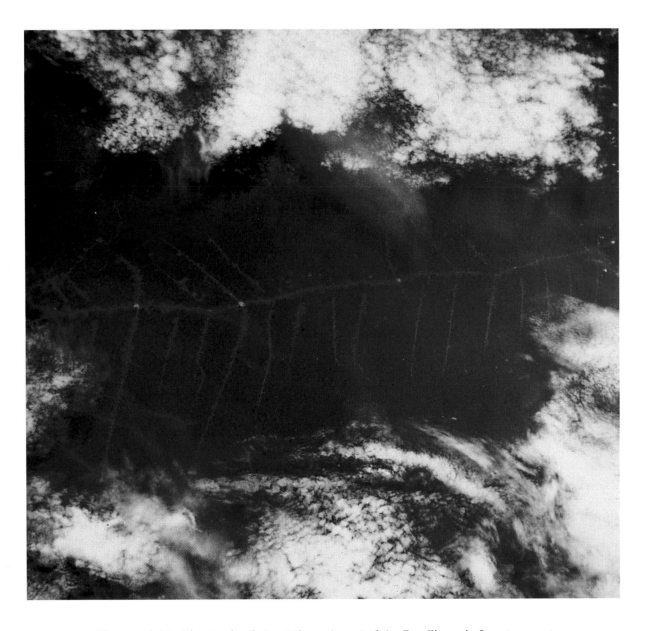

These weird-looking tracks that cut through part of the Brazilian rain forest are not caused by the movement of some strange animal; they are roads cut by people in the first stage of a giant forest-clearing exercise that will strip the country of vital vegetation.

been hoped for. They provided thousands of pictures to people all over the world. The U.S. government built stations in many countries to receive pictures directly from the satellite. In areas where hunger and lack of water often cause the deaths of thousands of people, the satellite pictures were particularly helpful. They showed people how satellites could bring information vital for better harvests. They gave people the means by which they could help improve food production and better manage the resources of their own countries.

This grid of small farm plots in Brazilian rain-forest clearings is prepared by the government so that peasants can rent land to grow crops, but it destroys the forest and much wildlife.

Several countries, including India, bought satellites from U.S. aerospace companies and paid NASA to launch them. These satellites provided direct monitoring specifically for the country concerned. Others continued to use Landsat data as more satellites were launched.

Landsat 2 followed in 1975, and *Landsat 3* in 1978. By this time, the first Landsat was no longer operating. Improvements to the instruments and the satellites made them increasingly valuable for gathering information about land and inland water areas.

Landsat 5 is prepared for launch from the Vandenberg Air Force Base in California using a rocket that will put the satellite into a polar orbit.

Interest in doing the same with ocean resources led to the development of *Seasat*. This satellite was designed to watch the world's oceans and provide information about waves, pollution, sea life, and other vital details people need to earn their living from the water. *Seasat* was launched in 1978 and performed well for only a few months before it failed. In the time it was operating, it sent back information that kept scientists busy for years.

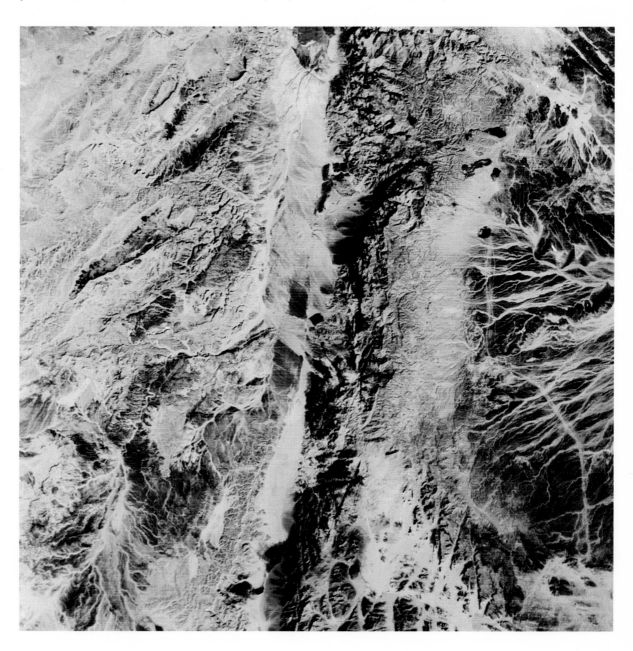

Seen from *Landsat 1* during January 1973, the deep canyon-like depression running from top to bottom divides Israel (left) from Jordan (right).

Meanwhile, plans went ahead for more Landsats, and an improved satellite was launched in 1982. This one was equipped with a more specific set of colors that helped distinguish one crop from another. Such detail was important for people who measure the total balance of several different crops over very large areas. Moreover, the resolution was considerably improved over the first Landsat launched ten years earlier. *Landsat 1* had a resolution of about 250 feet, while *Landsat 4* could see objects as small as 100 feet.

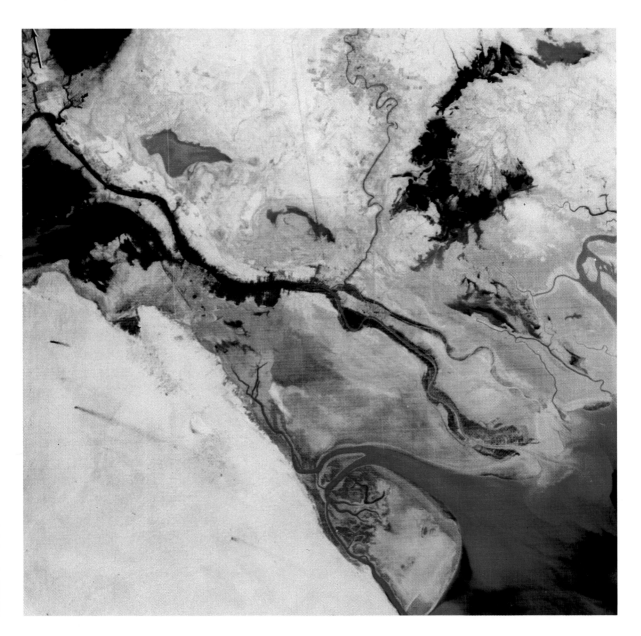

This picture, shot by Landsat in different colors of the spectrum, shows the place where the two famous rivers from the Bible, the Tigris and Euphrates, meet in Iraq.

Landsat 5 was similar to *Landsat 4* and was sent into space in 1984. Up to this time, the government had owned and operated Landsat. NASA designed and built the satellites and launched them from Vandenberg Air Force Base in California. The *National Oceanic and Atmospheric Administration, NOAA*, operated them and sold the data to people here and

Streets, roads, airfields, bridges, and islands can clearly be seen in this Landsat view of San Francisco Bay.

abroad. During the late 1980s, the Landsat program was turned over to a private company called Eosat. Eosat is designing replacement satellites that are even better than the first five Landsats, and will also be responsible for launching them.

In France, meanwhile, a satellite called *Spot* was launched by a European rocket in 1986. *Spot's* sensors and cameras were much better than Landsat's, and it could see objects as small

Seen by Landsat cameras in five separate bands of the color spectrum, Death Valley, California, comes dramatically alive with important information for scientists.

as 35 feet in size. That helped provide a wider range of information about small areas of land. *Spot* was particularly useful for discovering the distribution of crops and vegetation over areas where many small fields or farms are found.

Planet Watch

Long before the first remote sensing satellite had been launched, the United States Weather Service took an avid interest in using satellites for observing the atmosphere. Monitoring the weather and predicting what it will do several hours or days ahead is a complex and exacting task. Information is collected by many balloons in the air and buoys floating in the water; these provide details about pressure, temperature, and wind direction and strength. Satellites cannot replace all of this equipment, but they can help weather forecasters do a better job.

At first, satellites were sent up to orbit the Earth from low altitude and send back pictures of the clouds. As equipment became more sophisticated, additional information was obtained. This information included the level of moisture, the temperature in clouds, the precise movement of the wind, and the amount of rain falling on the ground. The first weather satellite was launched by NASA in 1960. Over the years the satellites got bigger, heavier, and better.

This color infra-red image of the Washington, D.C., area was taken by *Landsat 4* in November 1982, from a height of almost 440 miles.

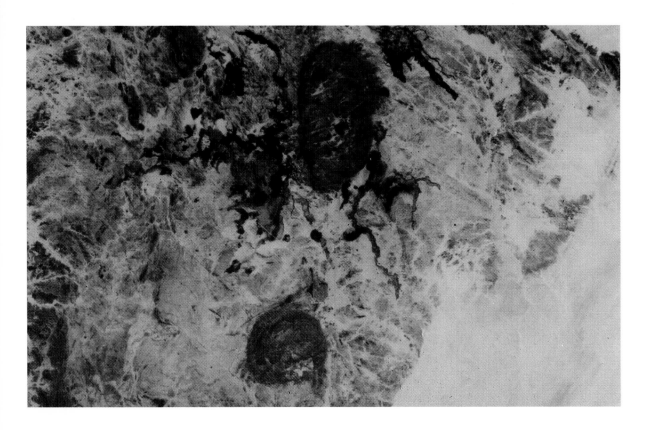

This color image from *Landsat 1* was taken in May 1973, from a height of 568 miles, and shows important surface features in Niger, North Africa.

Satellites have given storm warnings that have saved several thousand lives all over the world, and they are now a vital part of the forecaster's tools.

An even better weather watch was obtained when the first of a series of stationary satellites was launched in 1974. Like the military early-warning satellites 22,300 miles out in space, these weather satellites could take continuous pictures of one complete hemisphere of the Earth. These pictures improved the ability of weather forecasters to

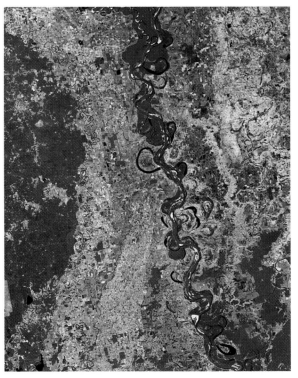

In this *Landsat 1* view of the Mississippi area, healthy crops, trees, and other green plants, which are very bright in the infra-red but invisible to the naked eye, are shown as bright red with towns and houses showing up as light pink.

watch the distant motion of hurricanes as they sped in from the oceans. Then the low-altitude satellites would zoom their cameras in on the local activity. Together, the two types of satellites provided a complete coverage of the world's weather.

Over the last fifteen years, the United States has worked cooperatively with several countries around the world to study and understand the weather on a global scale. Europe has launched several stationary weather satellites, and Japan, too, has begun a series of satellite launches specifically for monitoring weather in that part of the world. The Soviet Union also watches the weather and provides some level of cooperation with other countries. Information from these satellites is also useful in putting together theories about changes in the world's climate.

Information from different colors in the spectrum, viewed by special cameras aboard Landsat, tells specialists different things about the vegetation and crops on the ground, as indicated by this view of Holt County, Nebraska.

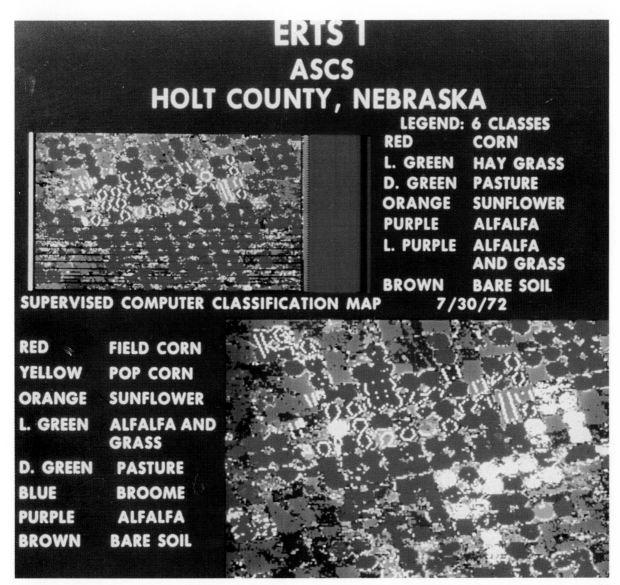

ERTS 1
ASCS
HOLT COUNTY, NEBRASKA

LEGEND: 6 CLASSES
RED   CORN
L. GREEN   HAY GRASS
D. GREEN   PASTURE
ORANGE   SUNFLOWER
PURPLE   ALFALFA
L. PURPLE   ALFALFA AND GRASS
BROWN   BARE SOIL

SUPERVISED COMPUTER CLASSIFICATION MAP   7/30/72

RED   FIELD CORN
YELLOW   POP CORN
ORANGE   SUNFLOWER
L. GREEN   ALFALFA AND GRASS
D. GREEN   PASTURE
BLUE   BROOME
PURPLE   ALFALFA
BROWN   BARE SOIL

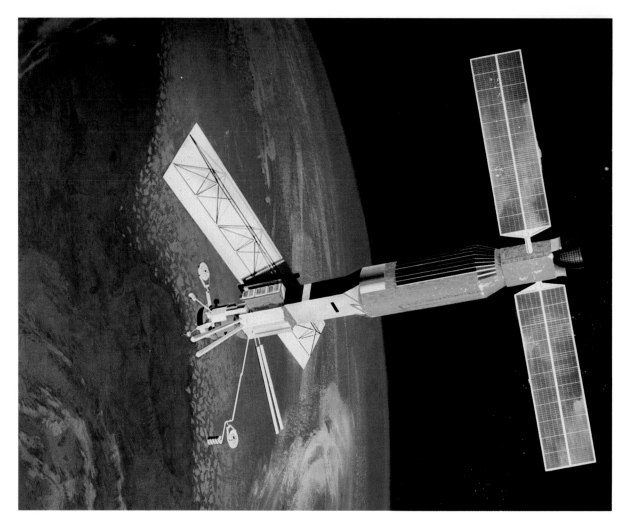

In an attempt to study the oceans and the seabed, NASA designed and built *Seasat* to help scientists better understand the nature of the world's oceans.

Many scientists now believe the Earth is getting slightly warmer each year. They believe that all the industrial waste we produce and the energy we burn is heating up the atmosphere above levels it would normally warm to. Waste creates heat because it decays and releases energy in the form of warm air. There is now solid evidence from satellites that this process has begun. Scientists are closely monitoring the precise rate of change so they can predict when it will begin to have serious effects.

One effect a hotter atmosphere will have on the Earth is that the ice at the north pole and the south pole will start to melt. This will increase the level of the sea. At first the level will rise by small amounts only, but eventually it will take over more and more of the low-lying land areas we use today for housing and industrial development. By combining the resources of Landsat pictures, low-altitude weather satellite shots, and high-orbiting stationary satellites, scientists will gather the information about how we can prevent the change from turning into a catastrophe.

We can change our wasteful ways and make more use of less energy. We have been wasteful

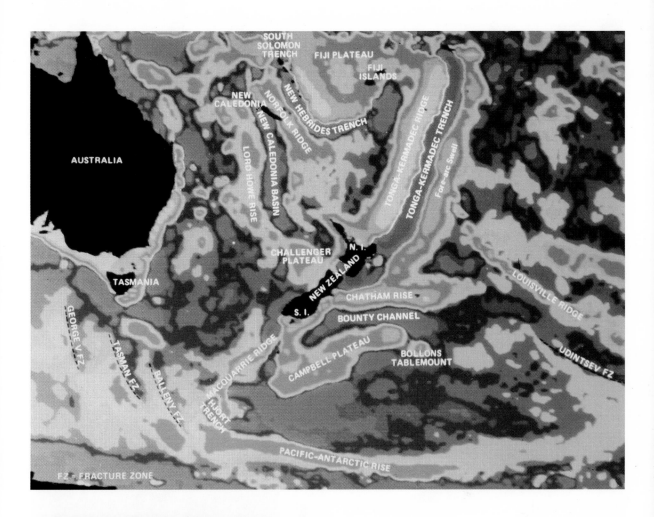

By using special radar, *Seasat* **was able to measure the flow of currents, the various changes in water temperature, and even features below the surface of the sea.**

and not at all wise in how we use our planet. We are tearing down the rain forests that provide water for crop growth and vegetation. We are polluting the atmosphere to the level where it will soon start to poison us. We are poisoning land and water with chemicals that destroy life. Satellites have brought this to our attention by providing information impossible to get by other means. What we do with the information is up to us.

Radar information from the *Seasat* **ocean observation satellite provides very accurate information on the height of surface features, generating a dramatic view of mountains and valleys.**

43

Spies in Space

During the 1960s, the military use of space for spying and watching other countries helped develop the technology for a series of civilian satellites that have helped people everywhere. When astronauts went to the moon, they looked back and spoke of the fragile bubble of life called Earth. Frank Borman sent a message from orbit around the moon at Christmas 1968, telling people everywhere about the "good Earth" he could see from space.

Since that time, scientists have built remarkable instruments for observing the Earth and improving the production of food, the health of crops, and the ability to warn of violent storms and dangerous weather. They have helped to lessen the threat to life and to give us information we need to look after our planet in a better way. But as humans, we also threaten ourselves. Our aggression sometimes leads to wars. Nuclear weapons make wars more likely to

A French satellite called *Spot* was launched in 1986 to provide views of the Earth's surface, which are sold to customers all over the world.

destroy vast groups of people not involved in the conflict. They threaten to pollute our planet with radiation.

In 1987 the leaders of the United States and the Soviet Union signed an agreement banning more than 4,000 nuclear warheads on missiles previously set up in Europe. That agreement would not have been possible without the sophisticated spy satellites that closely watch every activity in the U.S. and the Soviet Union. Without the ability of one side to monitor the

When Apollo astronauts went to the moon, they showed all of us on Earth how beautiful our planet looks from space. Only by using satellites to help us look after our planet can we prevent pollution and the destruction of green areas vital for the survival of many living things.

other, neither country would have signed the treaty. Even the military spy satellites that produced the technology to understand our planet better have played their part in making the planet a safer place for us all.

GLOSSARY

Ballistic missile	A rocket-propelled missile that flies under its own momentum and the force of gravity after its motor has been cut off.
Central Intelligence Agency (CIA)	The agency responsible for U.S. national security.
Early-warning satellites.	Satellites operated from very high orbits continuously watching the Earth for signs of surprise attacks by enemy missile forces.
Hallucinating	The belief by a person that he or she is seeing an object which in fact is not there.
Infra-red	The part of the electromagnetic spectrum with a longer wavelength than light but a shorter wavelength than radio waves. Like radio waves, infra-red radiation cannot be seen with the unaided human eye.
Multi-spectral scanner (MSS)	A satellite camera equipped with several different lenses, each viewing the same part of the Earth in a distinct color.
NASA	National Aeronautics and Space Administration, set up in October 1958 for the peaceful exploration of space.
NOAA	The National Oceanic and Atmospheric Administration, the U.S. government agency responsible for the scientific study and monitoring of oceans and the atmosphere.
Orbit	The curved path, usually almost circular, followed by a planet or satellite in its motion around another planet in space.
Polar orbit	An orbital path that takes a spacecraft over a planet or star's poles.
Remote sensing	Measurement and observation of land or the surface of another planet by examining reflected light or other forms of radiation.
Resolution	A photographic term used to indicate the technical capacity of a camera system to photograph small objects at long range.

INDEX

Page numbers in *italics* refer to photographs or illustrations.